Super Cheap Toronto Travel Guide 2020

Our Mission	5
Redefining Super Cheap	11
Discover Toronto	14
Planning your trip	16
Hack your Toronto Accommodation	18
The best price performance location in Toronto	24
Use our FREE	25
accommodation finder service	25
How to be a green tourist in Toronto	27
Saving money on Toronto Food	29
SNAPSHOT: How to Enjoy a $1,000 trip to Toronto for $120	30
Unique bargains I love in Toronto	31
How to use this book	32
OUR super cheap tips	33
Arriving	33
Getting around	34
Start with this free tour	36
See a Blue Jays game on the cheap	38
A cheaper Alternative to the CN Tower	39
Visit these Amazing Free museums	40
Go to the this amazing musical performance for free	42
Take the public ferry	43

Cheap theatre tickets	44
Go to the Beaches	45
Church Hop	46
Go Thrift shopping	47
Explore the BEST markets	49
Pack a picnic	50
Explore Street art	51
Visit this incredible district	52
Watch Free comedy	53
Visit Toronto Eaton Centre	53
Escape the crowds	54
Food and drink tips	55
Not super cheap but worth the fee	57
Is the tap water drinkable?	58
Haggle-o-meter	58
Need to Know	60
Cheapest route to Toronto from America	61
Cheapest route to Toronto from Europe	62
Cheap Eats	63
Avoid these tourist traps or scams	66
Getting Out	67
Personal Cost Breakdown	68
Toronto Streetcar Map	74

Thank you for reading	75
Bonus Budget Travel Hacks	78
How NOT to be ripped off	79
How to overcome travel related struggles	81
Car rental	84
You're sick	85
Where and How to Make Friends	88
GENERAL HACKS	90
CHEAP FLIGHT HACKS	93
Travel Gadgets	96
On The Road	98
Hacks for Families	103
Travel Gadgets for Families	106
How to earn money WHILE travelling	107
Safety	108
Our Writers	110
Copyright	111

Our Mission

Travel guides show you pricey accommodation and restaurants because they make money OFF OF YOU. Travel bloggers and influencers often do the same. Super Cheap Insider Guides help you use the system against itself to experience unforgettable trips that will blow your mind, not your budget.

We believe that travel can and is best enjoyed on a budget. We work to dispel myths, save you tons of money and help you find experiences that will flash before your eyes when you come to take your last breath on this beautiful earth.

Perhaps the biggest money saving trick you can employ is to know what you want to spend on and what you don't. This guide focuses on the cheap or free, but we do include the unique things to experience in our worth the fee section. There is little value in travelling somewhere and not experiencing all it has to offer. Where possible we've included cheap workarounds.

We are the first travel guide company to include Airbnb's in our recommendations if you think any of these need updating you can email me at philgtang@gmail.com

Who this book is for and why anyone can enjoy budget travel

Friends and family always ask me 'How can you afford to travel?' my response 'I have a unique skill and passion for finding bargains'. This doesn't mean I do any less or sleep in dirty hostels. Someone who spends A LOT on travel hasn't planned or wants to spend their money. I have formulated a system - which I hope to pass on to you in my travel guides - to juice everything from my travel adventures while spending the least possible money.

There is a difference between being cheap and frugal - I like to spend money on beautiful experiences, but 18 years of travel has taught me I could have a 20 cent experience that will stir my soul more than a $100 one. Of course, there are times when the reverse is true, my point is, spending money on travel is the best investment you can make but it doesn't have to be at levels set by hotels and attractions with massive ad spends and influencers who are paid small fortunes to get you to buy into something that you could have for a fraction of the cost.

Talking of 'the gram'. I've never used it, and probably never will though I have many friends who text me when they find good discounts on it or Twitter/Facebook, I love travelling so much because it forces me to be present-minded. I like to have the cold hard budget busting facts to hand (which is why I've included so many one page charts), but otherwise, I want to shape my own experience - and I'm sure you do too.

We have designed these travel guides to give you a unique planning tool to experience a soul-stirring trip without spending the ascribed tourist budget.

When it comes to FUN budget travel, it's all about what you know. You can have all the feels without most of the bills. An hour spent planning can save you hundreds on the same, maybe even thousands on the same experiences. Super Cheap Insider Guides have done the planning for you, so you can focus on what matters: immersing yourself in the sights, sounds and smells, meeting awesome people and most importantly, being relaxed and happy. My sincere hope is that my tips will bring you great joy at a fraction of the price most people recommend.

So, grab a cup of tea, put your feet up and relax; you're about to enter the world of enjoying Toronto on the cheap. Oh and don't forget a biscuit. You need energy to plan a trip of a lifetime on a budget.

Super Cheap Toronto is not for travellers with the following needs:

1. You require a book with detailed offline travel maps. Super Cheap Insider Guides are best used with Google Maps - download before you travel to make the most of your time and money.
2. You would like thousands of accommodation, food and attraction recommendations; by definition, cheapest is most often singular. We only include maximum value recommendations. We purposively leave out over-priced attractions when there is no workaround.
3. You would like detailed write-ups about hotels/Airbnbs/Restaurants. We are bargain hunters first and foremost. We dedicate our time to finding the best deals, not writing flowery language about their interiors. Plus things change. If I had a pound for every time I read a Lonely Planet description only to find the place totally different, I would be a rich man. Always look at online reviews for the latest up to date information.

If you want to save A LOT of money while comfortably enjoying an unforgettable trip to Toronto, minus the marketing, hype, scams and tourist traps read on.

Congratulations, you're saving money and doing Good!

We donate 10% of all book profits to charity.

This year we are donating to Animal Shelters including one in Toronto - TEAM Dog Rescue. The number of abandoned and homeless pets in Canada is estimated to be around 2 million. I'm sure you've seen your fair share of abandoned dogs during your travels: its heart wrenching to see man's best friend starving and alone.

'My dog Gracie was abandoned on the highway in Slovakia. At just ten months old, they tied her to the railings and left her there. Animal Hope picked her up and took care of her and found her a home with us. She is now a healthy, happy girl and loves travelling with us, getting her nose into new smells and soliciting belly rubs from fellow travellers. What breaks my heart is her 'I haven't been abandoned dance'. She is always so happy that we haven't abandoned her when we collect her from outside a su- supermarket that she dances on her leash for several minutes. Watch her 'I haven't been abandoned dance' dance   . Money could never buy the happiness she has brought my family and me, but donations can help other abandoned animals like her to find loving homes.'

Katherine Huber, a contributor to Super Cheap Vienna.

Donations are made on the 4th January of each year on profits from the previous year. To nominate a charity to receive 10% of the proceeds of sales from our 2020 editions complete the form here: supercheapinsiderguides.com

Gracie

Redefining Super Cheap

I grew up thinking you had to spend more than you could afford to have a good time travelling. Now I've visited many countries I know nothing is further from the truth. Before you embark upon reading our specific tips for Toronto. I want you to think about what you associate with the word cheap because you make your beliefs and your beliefs make you.

Here are the dictionary definitions of cheap:

1. costing very little; relatively low in price; inexpensive:
a cheap dress.
2. costing little labor or trouble:
Words are cheap.
3. charging low prices:
a very cheap store.
4. **of little account; of small value; mean; shoddy:**
cheap conduct; cheap workmanship.
5. **embarrassed; sheepish:**
He felt cheap about his mistake.
6. **stingy; miserly:**
He's too cheap to buy his own brother a cup of coffee.

Three out of six definitions have extremely negative connotations. The 'super cheap' we're talking about in this book is not shoddy, embarrassed or stingy. Hey, you've already donated to charity just by buying this book - how is that stingy? We added the super to reinforce our message. Super's dictionary definition stands for 'a super quality'. Super Cheap stands for enjoying the best on the lowest budget. Question other peoples definitions of cheap so you're not blinded to possibilities, potential, and prosperity. Here are some new associations to consider forging:

Shoddy

Cheap stuff doesn't last is an adage marketing companies have drilled into consumers. However by asking vendors the right questions cheap doesn't mean something won't last, I had a $10 backpack last for 8 years and a $100 suitcase bust on the first journey. A   out of San Francisco University found that people who spent money on experiences rather than things were happier. Memories last forever, not things, even expensive things. And as we will show you during this guide you don't need to pay to create great memories.

Embarrassed

I have friends who routinely pay more to vendors because they think their money is putting food on this person's table. Paradoxically, Cuban doctors are driving taxi's because they earn more money; it's not always a good thing for the place you're visiting to pay more and can cause unwanted distortion in their culture - Airbnb pushing out renters is an obvious example. Think carefully about whether the extra money is helping people or incentivising greed.

Stingy

Cheap can be eco-friendly. Buying thrift clothes is cheap but you also help the Earth. Many travellers are often disillusioned by the reality of traveling experience since the places on our bucket-lists are overcrowded. Cheap can take you away from the crowds. You can find balance and harmony being cheap. Remember,"A journey is best measured in friends, rather than miles." – Tim Cahill. And making friends is free!

Discover Toronto

Canada's largest city was founded in 1793 when it was first called York. The capital of Ontario boasts the best museums and art galleries in Canada. Its 5.6 million residents enjoy the finer things in life, plus the naturally beautiful nearby Toronto Islands and an abundance of green space - Ontario is larger than France and Spain combined.

Landmarks can be found all around the city, from the CN Tower - the centrepiece of the stunning skyline to Casa Loma, Toronto's famous castle. It's a cosmopolitan city with a laidback welcoming vibe. The city's diverse neighbourhoods; Toronto is home to large South Asian and Chinese communities celebrating different cultures with markets, delicious eateries and collaboration.

Toronto offers a wealth of opportunities to experience the city for free, from strolls through the city streets soaking up the spectacular architecture and statues, to a number of free museums, exhibitions, public buildings, parks and churches, tours as well as fabulous free entertainment, festivals ((like Pride, Caribana, Taste of the Danforth) and events but, like any city that caters to tourists, Toronto can be a budget-buster with Airbnbs averaging $120 a night, but take heart. The trick to keeping your trip affordable is to get off the tourist track and find the local deals. Let Toronto leave a lasting impression on your heart and mind, not your bank balance by following the advice in this guide. You could definitely get away with spending about $30 per person including accommodation.

Planning your trip

The best time to visit

If you are not tied to school holidays, the best time to visit is during the shoulder-season months from late April through May, and from mid-September through mid-October (Toronto's fall foliage is spectacular). The weather will be mild and there will be less crowds while the sidewalks will come to life with patio eateries, festivals, and markets. Mild weather does not arrive until late May so bring a coat if you plan to visit in spring.

If you plan to visit in winter bring layers and a waterproof coat, the temperature doesn't normally go below −20°C with snow from September or October to February or March.

Where to stay?

We stayed near Kensington Market, which was cheaper than other areas and still close enough to walk into the city. Toronto is bigger than you think and getting around is much easier the nearer you are, especially if you aren't visiting for long and want to see the main attractions.

The cheaper areas are:
- Chinatown
- Kensington Market
- AGO District.
- Queen West
- King West
- Liberty Village

The cheapest place to stay

We stayed in an Airbnb shared by four - https://www.airbnb.com/rooms/14874815?s=51 for $28 a night. The extremely well-reviewed **Planet Traveler Hostel** on Spadina and College is within walking distance to Chinatown and Kensington Market. They have dorm rooms from $25CAD per night and delicious free breakfast until 1pm. If you're travelling solo this is your best option, both for meeting people and saving pennies. If you're feeling for a night of luxury you can find same-day five star hotels on booking.com from $25. This only works on the weekends in the low season when hotels empty of their business travellers and only if you book the same day as your stay.

If you book at least 3 months in advance you can get an entire apartment to yourself on Airbnb for four people for $28 a night. Avoid the summer months when hosts use 'surge pricing' and airbnb prices triple.

Hack your Toronto Accommodation

Your two biggest expenses when travelling to Toronto are accommodation and food. This section is intended to help you cut these costs dramatically before and while you are in Toronto.

Hostels are the cheapest accommodation in Toronto but there are some creative workarounds to upgrade your stay on the cheap.

Use Time

There are two ways to use time. One is to book in advance. Three months will net you the best deal, especially if your visit coincides with an event. The other is to book on the day of your stay. This is a risky move, but if executed well, you can lay your head in a five-star hotel for a 2-star fee.

Before I travelled to Toronto, I checked for big events using a simple google search 'What's on in Toronto', there were no big events drawing travellers so I risked showing up with no accommodation booked (If there are big events on demand exceeds supply and you should avoid using this strategy) I started checking for discount rooms at 11 am using a private browser on booking.com.

Before I go into demand-based pricing, take a moment to think about your risk tolerance. By risk, I am not talking about personal safety. No amount of financial savings is worth risking that. What I am talking about is being inconvenienced. Do you deal well with last-minute changes? Can you roll with the punches or do you dislike it if something changes? Everyone is different and knowing yourself is the best way to plan a great trip. If you are someone that likes to have everything pre-planned using demand-based pricing to get cheap accommodation will not work for you. Skip this section and go to blind-booking.

Demand-based pricing

Be they an Airbnb host or hotel manager; no one wants empty rooms. Most will do anything to make some revenue because they still have the same costs to cover whether the room is occupied or not. That's why you will find many hotels drastically slashing room rates for same-day bookings.

How to book five-star hotels for a two-star price

You will not be able to find these discounts when the demand exceeds the supply. So if you're visiting during the peak season, or during an event which has drawn many travellers don't try this.

On the day of your stay, visit booking.com (which offers better discounts than Kayak and agoda.com). Hotel Tonight individually checks for any last-minute bookings, but they take a big chunk of the action, so the better deals come from booking.com. The best results come from booking between 2 pm and 4 pm when the risk of losing any revenue with no occupancy is most pronounced, so algorithms supporting hotels slash prices. This is when you can find rates that are not within the "lowest publicly visible" rate. To avoid losing customers to other websites, or cheapening the image of their hotel most will only offer the super cheap rates during a two hour window from 2 pm to 4 pm. Two guests will pay 10x difference in price but it's absolutely vital to the hotel that neither knows it.

Takeaway: To get the lowest price book on the day of stay between 2 pm and 4 pm and extend your search radius to include further afield hotels with good transport connections.

How to trick travel Algorithms to get the lowest hotel price

Do not believe anyone who says changing your IP address to get cheaper hotels or flights does NOT work. If you don't believe us, download a Tor Network and search for flights and hotels to one destination using your current IP and then the tor network (a tor browser hides your IP address from algorithms. It is commonly used by hackers). You will receive different prices.

The price you see is a decision made by an algorithm that adjusts prices using data points such as past bookings, remaining capacity, average demand and the probability of selling the room or flight later at a higher price. If booking.com knows you've searched for the area before it will keep the prices high. To circumvent this, you can either use a different IP address from a cafe or airport or data from an international sim. I use a sim from Three, which provides free data in many countries around the world. When you search from a new IP address, most of the time, and particularly near booking you will get a lower price. Sometimes if your sim comes from a 'rich' country, say the UK or USA, you will see higher rates as the algorithm has learnt people from these countries pay more. The solution is to book from a local wifi connection - but a different one from the one you originally searched from.

How to get last-minute discounts on owner rented properties

In addition to Airbnb, you can also find owner rented rooms and apartments on www.vrbo.com or HomeAway or a host of others. Nearly all owners renting accommodation will happily give renters a "last-minute" discount to avoid the space sitting empty, not earning a dime.

Go to Airbnb or another platform and put in today's date. Once you've found something you like start the negotiating by asking for a 25% reduction. A sample message to an Airbnb host might read:

Dear HOST NAME,

I love your apartment. It looks perfect for me. Unfortunately, I'm on a very tight budget. I hope you won't be offended, but I wanted to ask if you would be amenable to offering me a 25% discount for tonight, tomorrow and the following day? I see that you aren't booked. I can assure you, I will leave your place exactly the way I found it. I will put bed linen in the washer and ensure everything is clean for the next guest. I would be delighted to bring you a bottle of wine to thank you for any discount that you could offer.

If this sounds okay, please send me a custom offer, and I will book straight away.

YOUR NAME.

In my experience, a polite, genuine message like this, that proposes reciprocity will be successful 80% of the time. Don't ask for more than 25% off, this person still has to pay the bills and will probably say no as your stay will cost them more in bills than they make. Plus starting higher, can offend the owner and do you want to stay somewhere, where you have offended the host?

In Practice

To use either of these methods, you must travel light. Less stuff means greater mobility, everything is faster and you don't have to check-in or store luggage. If you have a lot of luggage, you're going to have fewer of these opportunities to save on accommodation. Plus travelling light benefits the planet - you're buying, consuming, and transporting less stuff.

Blind-booking

If your risk tolerance does not allow for last-minute booking, you can use blind-booking. Many hotels not wanting to cheapen their brand with known low-prices, choose to operate a blind booking policy. This is where you book without knowing the name of the hotel you're going to stay in until you've made the payment. This is also sometimes used as a marketing strategy where the hotel is seeking to recover from past issues. I've stayed in plenty of blind book hotels. As long as you choose 4 or 5 star hotels, you will find them to be clean, comfortable and safe. priceline.com, Hot Rate® Hotels and Top Secret Hotels (operated by lastminute.com) offer the best deals.

Hotels.com Loyalty Program

This is currently the best hotel loyalty program with hotels in Toronto. The basic premise is you collect 10 nights and get 1 free. hotels.com price match, so if booking.com has a cheaper price you can get hotel.com, to match. If you intend to travel more than ten nights in a year, its a great choice to get the 11th free.

Don't let time use you.

Rigidity will cost you money. You pay the price you're willing to pay, not the amount it requires a hotel to deliver. Therefore if you're in town for a big event, saving money on accommodation is nearly impossible so in such cases book three months ahead.

The best price performance location in Toronto

A room near down-town Toronto where the attractions, restaurants, and nightlife are within walking distance will save you time on transport but restaurants and bars get much cheaper the further you go from famous tourist attractions. You will also get a better idea of the day to day life of a local if you stay in a neighbourhood like Etobicoke. It depends on the Toronto you want to experience. For the tourist experience stay in the centre either in a last-minute hotel or Airbnb. For a taste of local life the leafy district of Etobicoke is the best you will find. EST Hotel in Etobicoke is a luxurious 4 star hotel with consistent rooms from $40 a night.

Use our FREE accommodation finder service

Feeling overwhelmed by all the accommodation options? Save yourself stress, hassle and time by using our FREE accommodation finder service.

We pride ourselves on actively helping our readers find the best price-performance accommodation. We normally charge $50 for this service, but for our paid readers it is FREE when you leave an honest review of this book. (Just a few short words like 'Excellent budget tips and insider insights' is all it takes).

So, how do you use the service?

Simply send our Services Manager, Amy Abraham the following information:

1. A screenshot proof of purchase. (Go to your Amazon account, and click orders and make a screenshot of your purchase.)
2. Send a screenshot of your review of the guide on Amazon.
3. And answers to the following questions:

- What's your Budget? (e.g. lowest possible)
- How many are travelling and what are their ages?
- What Approximate location do you desire? (e.g. as close to the centre as possible/ near public transport)
- Do you have a strong dislike of either hostels or Airbnbs?

- If anyone in your group has mobility restrictions/ requires a lift/ no stairs etc?
- Add any details you think are pertinent to your needs.

About Amy and her team

Amy has travelled to over 170 countries personally and has recruited a team of bargain hunters to provide our accommodation finder service.

Send your details via E-mail to Amy Abraham at Amy@supercheapinsiderguides.com

What you'll receive

Amy and her team will work their magic. Within 24 hours you will be sent a list of the top three accommodations for your specific needs prioritised by which one we recommend.

We offer the same service for finding you the cheapest most direct flight. See our cheapest route to Toronto for details.

If you would like to follow us on Facebook you can find us here: https://www.facebook.com/SuperCheapInsiderGuides/ . We also accept accommodation search requests via Facebook messenger, just make sure you send the necessary information listed above.

(Please note: If you received this book for free as part of a promotion, we cannot extend this service to you.)

How to be a green tourist in Toronto

Like other major cities Toronto battles with air pollution. Thankfully levels of the five most common air pollutants have been steadily decreasing. Still as our climate grapples with increased travel its important as responsible tourists that we help not hinder Toronto. There is a bizarre misconception that you have to spend money to travel in an eco-friendly way. This like, all marketing myths was concocted and hyped by companies seeking to make money off of you. In my experience, anything with eco in front of their names e.g Eco-tours will be triple the cost of the regular tour. Don't get me wrong sometimes its best to take these tours if you're visiting endangered areas, but normally such places have extensive legislation that everyone, including the eco and non-eco tour operators must comply with. The vast majority of ways you can travel eco-friendly are free and even save you money:

- Avoid Bottled Water - get a good water bottle and refill. The water in Toronto is safe to drink.
- Thrift shop but check the labels and don't buy polyester clothes - overtime plastic is released into the ocean when we wash polyester.
- Don't put it in a plastic bag, bring a cotton tote with you when you venture out.
- Pack Light - this is one of the best ways to save money. If you find a 5-star hotel for tonight for $10, and you're at an Airbnb or hostel, you can easily pack and upgrade hassle-free. A light pack equals freedom and it means less to wash.
- Travel around Toronto on Bikes or e-Scooters or use Public Transportation.
- Car Pool with services like Uber/Lyft share.
- Walk, this is the best way to get to know Toronto intimately. You never know what's around the corner.
- Travel Overland - this isn't always viable especially if you only have limited time off work, but where possible avoid

flying and if you have to compensate by off-setting or keeping the rest of your trip carbon-neutral by doing all of the above.

Saving money on Toronto Food

Breakfast

If you stay somewhere with a free breakfast, eat smart. Don't eat sugary cereals or white flour rich pastries if you don't want to be hungry an hour later. Before leaving your hotel or checking out, find some fresh fruit, water, and granola in the fitness centre or coffee in the lobby or business centre. If your hotel doesn't have free breakfast, don't take it. You can always eat cheaper outside. Karine's on McCaul Street has the best cheap breakfast we found in Toronto.

Visit supermarkets at discount times.

You can get a 50 per cent discount around 5 pm at the Sobeys supermarkets on fresh produce. The cheaper the supermarket, the less discounts you will find, so check Sobeys at 5 pm before heading to value markets. Some items are also marked down due to sell-by date after the lunchtime rush so its also worth to check in around 3 pm.

Use delivery services on the cheap.

Take advantage of local offers on food delivery services. Most platforms including Foodora offer $10 off the first order in Toronto.

SNAPSHOT: How to Enjoy a $1,000 trip to Toronto for $120

(full breakdown at the end of the guide)

Stay	entire apartment $28 https://www.airbnb.com/rooms/14874815?s=51 divided by four people $7 a night - book ahead. Hostel $25 a night for a dorm bed with free breakfast or use our accommodation finder service.
Eat	Cheap eats and food trucks
Move	Bike hire $15.
See	Free attractions, beaches, neighbourhoods, architecture, free walking tour.
Total	US$120

Unique bargains I love in Toronto

Toronto has the reputation of being an expensive destination. Fortunately, some of the best things in life are free (or almost free): hiking, cycling, swimming, fishing, and you can find cheap hockey, baseball, basketball tickets. Plus there are a plethora of community centres with subsidized activities: yoga, to painting and learning to code. Thrift shopping in Toronto is a must! And you can refuel after a hard day of bargain hunting on delicious cheap eats. Then you've the energy to visit visit museums on their free days/evenings - saving more bucks!

The first thing you should do when you arrive is check https://www.toronto.com/free-events/ to see what free events are on.

How to use this book

Google and Tripadvisor are your on-the-go guides while travelling, a travel guide adds the most value during the planning phase, and if you're without wifi. Always download the google map for your destination - having an offline map will make using this guide much more comfortable. For ease of use, we've set the book out the way you travel starting with arriving, how to get around, then on to the money-saving tips. The tips we ordered according to when you need to know the tip to save money, so free tours and combination tickets feature first. We prioritised the rest of the tips by how much money you can save and then by how likely it was that you would be able to find the tip with a google search. Meaning those we think you could find alone are nearer the bottom. I hope you find this layout useful. If you have any ideas about making Super Cheap Insider Guides easy to use, please email me philgattang@gmail.com . Now let's get started with juicing the most pleasure from your trip to Toronto with the least possible money.

OUR super cheap tips

Arriving

Toronto airport is a long way from the city. A cab can cost you $75. Save your money, take the UB EXPRESS TRAIN train for $12 - the cheapest way to the city. It takes 25 minutes from the airport to Union Station in downtown Toronto and the train departs every 15 minutes.

Getting around

The Toronto metro has two lines. If you need to get somewhere not on them use the streetcars. Get a PRESTO card and it will cost you $2.90 per ride.

Cycle: Toronto is a lovely city to walk or cycle in the warmer months. Like a growing number of cities around the world, Toronto has a bike-sharing program, and there are stations everywhere and many new cycle paths. You pay $15 for a 3 day pass. https://bikesharetoronto.com/

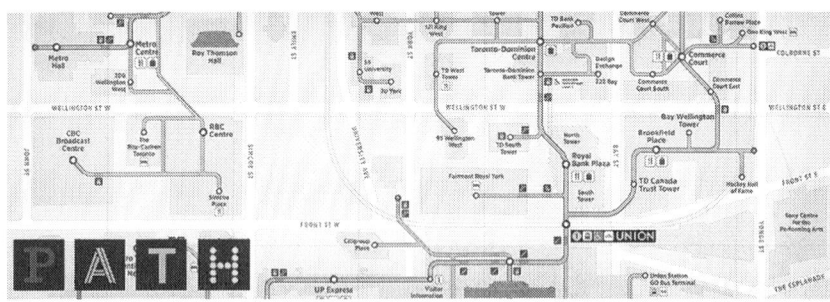

 INSIDER CULTURAL INSIGHT

The city's underground PATH network is over 30km and is used by over 300,000 people daily to go to and from work.

Walk – it's the best way to discover and most of the attractions are close together. If your travelling in winter use The PATH - an underground pedestrian walkway network in downtown Toronto that spans more than 30 kilometres of restaurants, shopping, services and entertainment.

Get around for FREE
Use ride sharing service Lyft. Google for a free credit and open a new Lyft account. Toronto offers up to $50 free credit, which could cover your transport for your whole trip.

💡 INSIDER INSIGHT

If cycle keep an eye out for three white dots on the floor at intersections. They detect when you approach on your bike to signal the traffic lights to change.

Start with this free tour

Glenn Gould - the most-celebrated classical pianist of the 20th century.

Forget exploring Toronto by wandering around aimlessly. Start with a free organised tour. Nothing compares to local advice, especially when travelling on a budget. Ask for their recommendations for the best cheap eats, the best bargains, the best markets, the best place for a particular street eat. Perhaps some of it will be repeated from this guide, but it can't hurt to ask, especially if you have specific needs or questions. At the end you should leave an appropriate tip (usually around $5), but nobody bats an eye lid if you are unable or unwilling to do so, tell them you will leave a good review and always give them a little gift from home - I always carry small Vienna fridge magnets and I always tip the $5, but it is totally up to you.

This is the free tour I did. I thought it was a great introduction to the city and covered the main attractions. You can book here: https://www.tourguys.ca/toronto-free-walking-tours/

A note on paying for tours

The only time paying for a tour is worth it, is when you couldn't reach the place without the tour (e.g you need a boat), or when the tour is about the same price as the attraction entry. Otherwise you can do a range of self-guided tours using gpsmycity.com for FREE.

💡 INSIDER MONEY SAVING INSIGHT

Try Geocaching

This is where you hunt for hide-and-seek containers. You need a mobile device to follow the GPS clues in Toronto. A typical cache is a small, waterproof container with a logbook where you can leave a message or see various trinkets left by other cache hunters. Build your own treasure hunt by discovering geocaches in Toronto. www.geocaching.com

See a Blue Jays game on the cheap

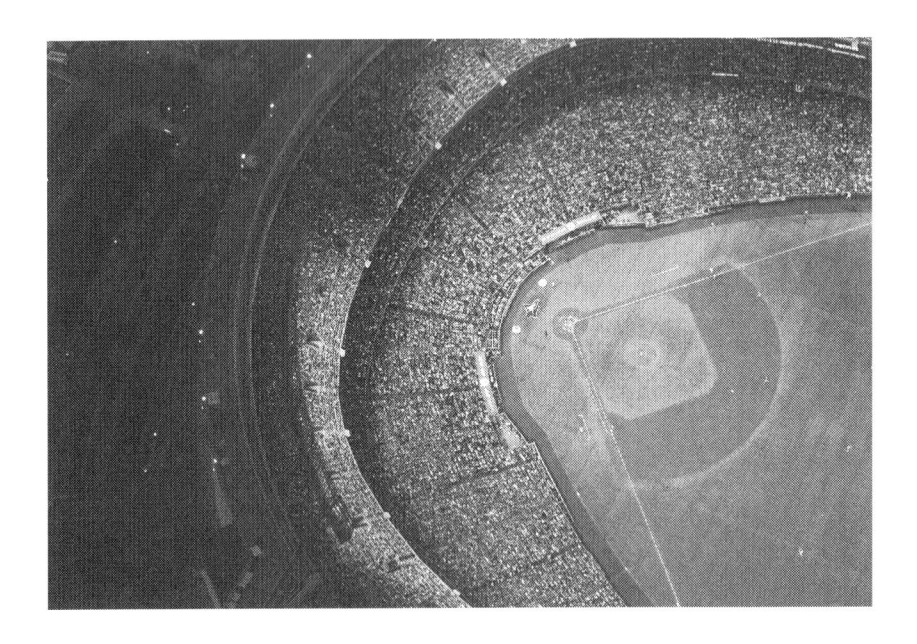

The Toronto Blue Jays are a Canadian professional baseball team who compete in Major League Baseball. The team plays its home games at the Rogers Centre. You can grab a ticket for $5 when you book early. The atmosphere is electric. The 5$ beer is a small can still best price for sport centres. And the meals are actually quite large for 5$. Visit https://www.tickpick.com/toronto-blue-jays-tickets/

A cheaper Alternative to the CN Tower

While CN tower charges $36 for admission, there are places that give visitors a **free view of the Toronto skyline:** The Chester Hill lookout, 10 minutes walk from Broadview subway station has a 180-degree view of the CN Tower. Riverdale Park on Broadview Avenue is another place to view the Toronto downtown skyline. It has a huge green space in the forefront for walking, relaxing, picnicking, and watching the sunset all for free.

Visit these Amazing Free museums

Many of Toronto's top museums are free and others have free entry times. Here are the best of the crop you can visit, with the free times saving you $40!

Permanent Collection of the Art Gallery of Ontario is free from 6 to 8:30 p.m. on Wednesdays.

Bata Shoe Museum operate a pay-what-you-wish admission is held every Thursday evening between 5 to 8 p.m.

Museum of Contemporary Canadian Art (MOCCA) is pay-what-you-can at all times.

The Market Gallery at St. Lawrence Market explores Toronto history and culture and is always free.

The Art Gallery of Ontario is free between 6 and 8:30pm on Wednesday evenings.

Go to the this amazing musical performance for free

Pack a lunch and attend one of the Canadian Opera Company's free lunch hour performances. They are the largest opera company in Canada and one of the largest producers of opera in North America. Check their website for dates and times: https://www.coc.ca/

Address: 145 Queen St W, Toronto, ON M5H 4G1, Canada

Take the public ferry

Get a unique view of Toronto by taking the public ferry to Hanlans Point. Its much less busy than Centre island and costs $7.50 return. 90% less than any boat tour catering to tourists. For departure points and times visit https://www.-torontoisland.com/ferry.php

Cheap theatre tickets

ToTix offers heavily discounted tickets for day-of-show performances. The best discounts are had in person at the southeast corner of Young-Dundas Square but you can also check their website on the day: https://www.todaytix.com/x/toronto/shows

Go to the Beaches

'Beaches' is a neighbourhood is a stretch of beaches. Go for a stroll along **Woodbine Beach** a Blue Flag beach that is extremely popular in summer. You'll find the start of the Boardwalk, which stretches out for 3km and is loved by runners.

Church Hop

Not only exceptional architecturally and historically, Toronto's churches contain exquisite art, artefacts and other priceless treasures. Best of all, entry to general areas within them is, in most cases, free. Have a look inside **St. James' Cathedral,** the Gothic-style house of worship you see here today was opened back in 1853 and stands on the site of Toronto's first church. Marvel at the beautiful collection of stained glass windows while you're there. Do respect the fact that although many of the places of worship are also major tourist attractions, People come here to pray and celebrate significant events on religious calendars as part of their daily lives.

Go Thrift shopping

Value Village

Thrift stores also known as charity shops or second hand shops are treasure troves in Toronto. The Yonge Street Mission - Double Take Store, Value Village and St John's Thrift Store were the best bang for your buck thrift stores I found in the city. If you want to do further hunting, what you want to look for are the ones located in affluent areas with low-income foot-fall. If you're not familiar with the area and asking around hasn't returned any results, here's what you can do. Google for the most expensive area to live in Toronto you are visiting, sometimes they are a little outside the city. Then put the American term Thrift store into

Google Maps. Start with the most expensive and work your way through until the middle-tier ones. You will be surprised what you find.

Explore the BEST markets

Kensington Market is a warren of narrow streets that will take you back in time. The market opened in 1815, as you walk amongst its friendly faces you can imagine horse and cart traders. Here you can sample old world pastries and browse the racks of vintage clothing.

For the cheapest markets in Toronto head to the chinatowns, there are three chinatowns in Toronto. The first in Kensington Market, the second in Broadview Avenue and the third is in Sacrbourgh which is on the outskirts.

Pack a picnic

The cost of eating out can quickly add up. For a meal that doesn't break the bank pack a picnic to enjoy in a park with a blanket and a bottle of fizz. Queen's Park is the perfect place to escape the city. It was built in 1860 and dedicated to Queen Victoria, it's also the site of the Ontario Legislative Building.

Or there is High Park, the largest park in Toronto has a huge array of attractions for you to enjoy, visit the free mini-zoo, stroll around Grenadier Pond or check out the Chinese Gardens.

If you're into nature, check out the **Allan Gardens Conservatory** It is a large Victorian-style conservatory home to a huge collection of plants such as palm trees, cacti and all kinds of flowers. Open daily 10am-5pm.

You can also visit a secret Japanese garden located within the University of Toronto's Terrence Donnelly Centre for Cellular and Biomolecular Research. This is a beautiful paradise offering visitors peace and tranquility.

Explore Street art

Graffiti alley (just put that into google maps) is full of colorful murals and graffiti art. Some of the most beautiful and iconic pieces are here. Murals sometimes cover up entire buildings and symbolize recent and historical events and topics.

Visit this incredible district

Distillery District

The pedestrian-only Distillery District is set in quaint 19th century buildings which once housed a large whiskey distillery. Browse the free galleries including Corkin Gallery and Thompson Landry Gallery and the outdoor sculptures.

Watch Free comedy

Comedy Bar is a Comedy club offering free improv and stand-up shows from new and established performers on Wednesday nights.
Address: 945 Bloor St W
Opens 6PM

Visit Toronto Eaton Centre

This historic mall has a huge array of shops, clothiers and restaurants housed under a glass ceiling.

Escape the crowds

If you are easily overwhelmed by crowds visit the obvious attractions as early as possible, peak people flow is 11 am to 5 pm so get up early to enjoy the attractions serenely. Luckily Toronto also has many hidden gems that aren't commercialised or too crowded most of the time. Here are the best:

1. Take the ferry, you can get off at either Ward's island or Hanlan's Islands and snap some Skyline photos from Toronto Islands.
2. Explore an alley packed with colourful murals. Graffiti alley starts at Rush Lane.
3. Sugar Beach is a whimsical 8,500-square-metre beach park, it takes its name from a sugar factory next to it.
4. Cycle through Gates Gully Scarborough. You'll find Bluffers Park, the Rosetta McClain Gardens, and Port Union Waterfront Park and the unofficial nude beaches.

Food and drink tips

Free coffee refill
If you need a laptop day head to any of these coffee shops with unlimited free coffee refills: ON - Dark Horse Espresso, Almond Butterfly Cafe and Bakeshop, Mitzi's Café, HotBlack Coffee, Fiorentina or YAYA coffee shops. Moon beam is the best and cheapest coffee shop in the city but no refills.

Eat in Little Tokyo
While in Toronto you have to try Uncle Tetsu's Japanese Cheesecake and all the other yummy and cheap Japanese food in Little Tokyo. It would be crazy to leave Toronto without a Little Tokyo in your belly.

Best bang for your buck all-you-can-eat
Spring Sushi is an all-you-can-eat loved by locals. You pay $20 for lunch - https://springsushi.com/toronto/menu/all-you-can-eat-menu/ All you can eat buffets are a great way to stock on on nutritious food while travelling. Dishes like fish are normally expensive, but here you can chow down on your omega 3's for much less. Don't drink much water or eat bread and you'll get more than your money's worth.
Address: 10 Dundas St E #4.

Find deals to eat out
Great sites to visit include Yelp Deals, Groupon, LivingSocial, and Valpak. You can also find coupons at places such as your local hotel, bus or train stations, and the airport, so keep your eyes open.

Nightlife – Bars and Clubs

If you don't go out you'll miss out on some great venues – the clubs and bars make it hard to catch some sleep in Toronto but be Wide Open has very cheap drinks ($4 for every drink) it can get pretty busy but the bartenders are very friendly.
Address: 139A Spadina Ave, Toronto, ON M5V 2L7, Canada

Other cheap joints with no cover charge include: The Bar With No Name. Bistro 422. Bathurst Local 322. Sneaky Dee's. Green Room. Done Right Inn and The Lab.

Not super cheap but worth the fee

Check groupon.com/toronto for deals on all these attractions.

Ripley's Aquarium of Canada
Adult – $32.00. Youth (6-13) – $22.00. Child (3-5) – $10.00
Expansive, modern aquarium with many species and habitats on display.

Casa Loma
Adult $27
Though it never housed royalty (The house was built in 1914 by Sir Henry Pellat, a financier who made his fortune providing electricity to Toronto but then went broke) this gothic-revival-style mansion and garden makes for an interesting afternoon.

Toronto Zoo
Adult $23
Immense zoo with outdoor pavilions housing hundreds of species, plus a large botanical collection.

Is the tap water drinkable?

Yes.

Haggle-o-meter

How much can you save haggling here?

Gentle haggling is common at markets in Toronto. Haggling in stores is generally unacceptable, although some good-humoured bargaining at smaller artisan or craft shops is cool if you are making multiple purchases.

Websites to save you Money

1. TalkTalkbnb.com - Here you stay for free when you teach the host your native language
2. Rome2Rio.com - the go to site for good travel prices on train, bus, planes etc. Especially good for paths less travelled.
3. couchsurfing.com - stay for free with a local - always check reviews.
4. trustedhousesitter.com - always check reviews
5. booking.com - now sends you vouchers for discounts in the city when you book through them
6. airbnb.com for both accommodation and experiences.
7. hostelbookers.com - book hostels
8. https://www.groupon.com/local/toronto
9. **https://www.toronto.com/free-events/ - Take advantage of free events**
10. https://www.eventbrite.ca/d/canada--toronto/free-yoga/ - Free yoga
11. http://www.torontofreeparking.ca/ if driving use the free parking map

Need to Know

Currency: Canadian dollar

Language: Toronto .

Money: Widely available ATMs. Beware American Express might not work here.

Visas: http://www.doyouneedvisa.com/

Time: GMT - 8

When to Go

High Season: July and August.

Shoulder: May, April, June

Low Season: September to May.

Important Numbers

911

Watch to understand the History

Toronto's history is fascinating. There are tons of documentaries. This is a great one - https://www.youtube.com/watch?v=RnTTQlrg9W4

Cheapest route to Toronto from America

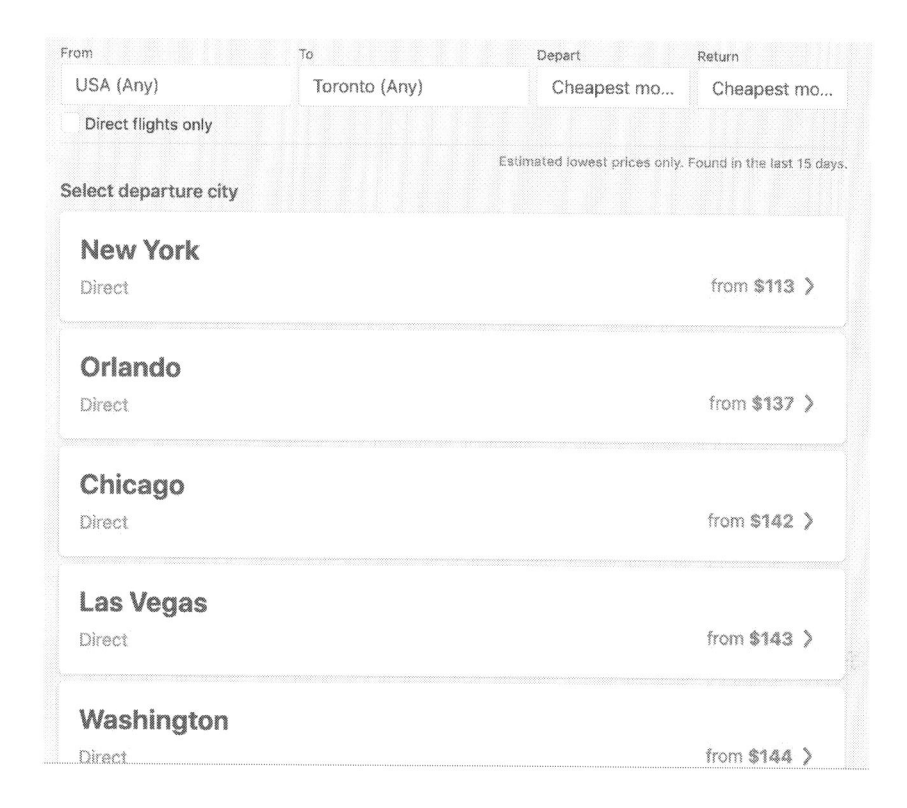

From	To	Depart	Return
USA (Any)	Toronto (Any)	Cheapest mo...	Cheapest mo...

☐ Direct flights only

Estimated lowest prices only. Found in the last 15 days.

Select departure city

New York
Direct — from **$113** >

Orlando
Direct — from **$137** >

Chicago
Direct — from **$142** >

Las Vegas
Direct — from **$143** >

Washington
Direct — from **$144** >

At the time of writing Spirt are flying to Toronto direct for around $100. I specialise in finding cheap flights, so if you need help finding a cheap flight simply review this book and send me an email. philgtang@gmail.com (Please send me a screenshot of your review - with your flight hacking request). I aim to reply to you within 12 hours. If it's an urgent request mark the email URGENT in the subject line and I will endeavour to reply ASAP.

Cheapest route to Toronto from Europe

At the time of writing West Jet are flying to Toronto direct for around $300 return from the UK. I specialise in finding cheap flights, so if you need help finding a cheap flight simply review this book and send me an email. philgtang@gmail.com (Please send me a screenshot of your review - with your flight hacking request). I aim to reply to you within 12 hours. If it's an urgent request mark the email URGENT in the subject line and I will endeavour to reply ASAP.

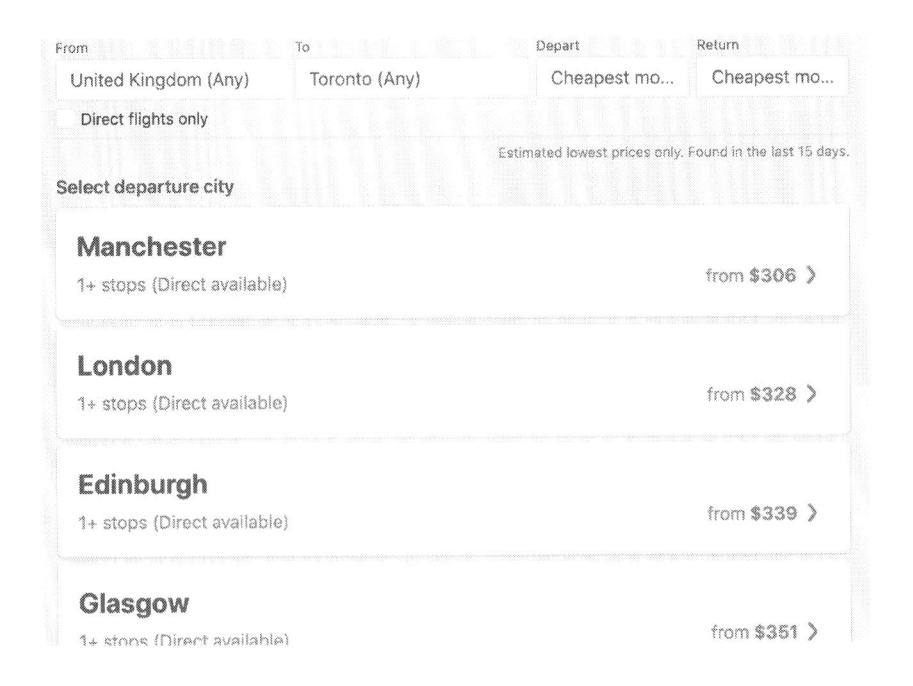

From	To	Depart	Return
United Kingdom (Any)	Toronto (Any)	Cheapest mo...	Cheapest mo...

Direct flights only

Estimated lowest prices only. Found in the last 15 days.

Select departure city

Manchester
1+ stops (Direct available) — from $306 ⟩

London
1+ stops (Direct available) — from $328 ⟩

Edinburgh
1+ stops (Direct available) — from $339 ⟩

Glasgow
1+ stops (Direct available) — from $351 ⟩

Cheap Eats

Fill your stomach without emptying your wallet by trying these local eats with mouth-watering main dishes under $8.

(Download the offline map on google maps, (instructions 1. go to app 2. select offline apps in the left sidebar 3. go to the area you want to download 4. click download). Then simply type the restaurant names in to navigate, star them so you can see where the cheap eats are when you're out and about to avoid wasting your money at hyped tourist joints)

When The Pig Came Home Delicatessen
Eating a jerk chicken sandwich from this place was the best $5 I spent in Toronto.

Seven Lives
Great, large tacos at an affordable price ($6). Cash-only taqueria fixing up Baja-style tacos and seafood in a trendy Kensington Market storefront.

Mystic Muffin
No-frills counter serve with renowned apple cake, offering baked goods and Lebanese-inspired lunches. The bagels with coffee are great and very cheap - $6.

Rasta Pasta
Cheap delicious Jamaican food.

Manpuku Japanese Eatery
Noodle house hideaway in a food court delivers a modern and unique take on Japanese comfort food.

Banh Mi Boys

Asian-inspired subs, sandwiches, tacos and steamed buns spiced to order in a snug and lively location. One of the best cheap sandwich joints in Toronto.

Loga's Corner
Delicious dumplings, Super friendly owners and cheap prices - $6.

Jumbo Empanadas
Chilean eatery offering meat and vegetable empanadas.

Gale's Snack Bar
Great greasy spoon fare (Sandwiches and milkshakes) at prices that would have been cheap 25 years ago

Salad King
Thai eatery serving noodles, curries and salads, with communal tables and a choice of spice levels.

Tortería San Cosme
Colorful spot with a counter made up like a street-food stall dishing out Mexican sandwiches.

Messini Authentic Gyros
Simple Mediterranean spot for Greek sandwiches, very popular with the late-night crowd.

El Furniture Warehouse
Cool, simple dive bar with lots of exposed wood and a classic pub-grub menu with nothing over $5.

Completo
Small South American sandwich shop with creative combos and bright graffiti on the walls and a patio.

LASA by Lamesa
Cheap Filipino meats, seafood and stews.

Saffron Spice Kitchen
Classic Indian dishes and takeout, with a few tables and low prices.

Govinda's
Set in a historic building, this modest eatery offers a buffet of vegetarian Indian food for $8.

Avoid these tourist traps or scams

Toronto prides itself on being a welcoming city but there are two scams to be mindful of:

Accommodation rental scams

Some people are taking pictures of real rental properties and hotel rooms and using them to create fake adverts. If using Airbnb, be sure to check for:

- a track record of good reviews - and not all left on the same day/week
- a good location relative to public transportation in which you can easily get to the city.

Distraction thefts on street cars

Be aware of your valuables and stow your luggage so that you can see it. If someone stops to speak to you be aware that they could trying to distract you so that an accomplice can steal your stuff.

Getting Out

Bus

You can get the bus to Niagara Falls for $5 with Megabus. Check megabus.com for other cheap onward destinations from Toronto and book ahead to get the lowest prices.

Plane

At the time of writing Air Transat are offering the cheapest flights onwards. Take advantage of discounts and specials. Sign up for e-newsletters from local carriers including Air Transat to learn about special fares. Be careful with cheap airlines, most will allow hand-luggage only, and some charge for anything that is not a backpack. Check their

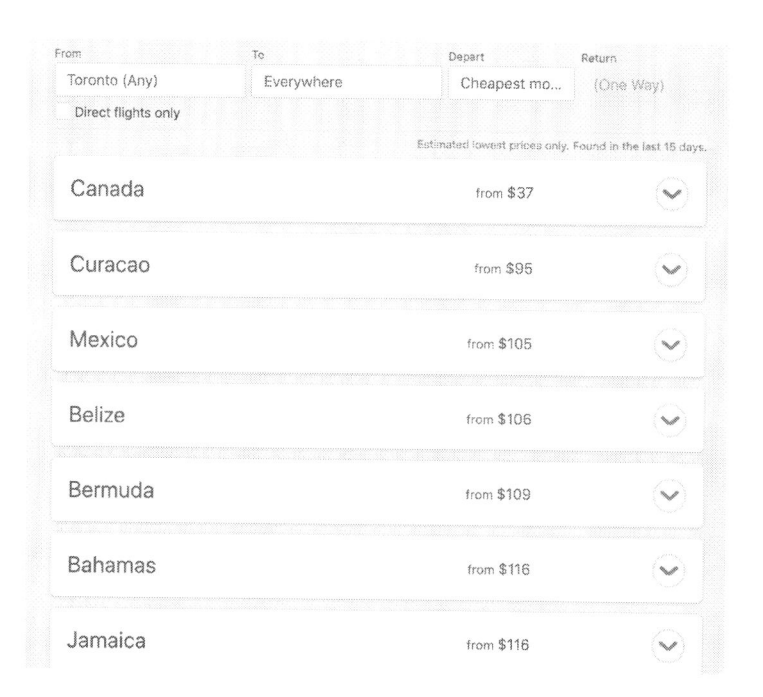

From	To	Depart	Return
Toronto (Any)	Everywhere	Cheapest mo...	(One Way)

☐ Direct flights only

Estimated lowest prices only. Found in the last 15 days.

Canada	from $37
Curacao	from $95
Mexico	from $105
Belize	from $106
Bermuda	from $109
Bahamas	from $116
Jamaica	from $116

websites before booking if you need to take luggage.

Personal Cost Breakdown

	How	Cost normally	Cost when following suggested tip
How I got from the airport to the city	$12 train from the airport	$35 Taxi	$12 (I got the bus out so didn't need to go back to the airport)
Where I stayed	airbnb in the city - split between four.	Hotels are upwards of $150 a night.	$7 a night
Tastiest street foods I ate and cost	Everything in Little Tokyo.	You don't need to spend more than $5 - $8 to eat well in Toronto.	$5
How I got around	Walked, cycled and used Lyft.	$50	$10 ferry ride $15 bike fees
What I saw and paid	Beaches, free museums, skyscapers, parks, markets	There's so many AMAZING things to do and see in Toronto.	$15 on shop brought beers
My onward flight	Bus to Nigara falls	Book ahead for the lowest prices.	$5
My Total costs			US$120

RECAP: How to have a $1,000 trip to Toronto on a $120 budget

Five star hotels
Last minute 5 star hotels deals. Check on the same day of your stay for cheap five star hotel deals. Go to booking.com enter Toronto, tonight, only one night and filter by 5 stars. This can be very effective on the weekends when hotels empty of their business travellers but only works in the low season/ end of season for sporting events.
Potential saving $800.

Restaurant deals
Nearly every restaurant in Toronto offers a midday menu for lunch at around $6 If you're on a budget, but like eating out, consider doing your dining in the daytime.
Potential saving $100.

Go to museums/ attractions on their free days
Get cultured for free, or for cheap, by knowing the gallery and museum discount days. The average traveller spends $100 on museums/ attractions in Toronto but there's an abundance of free or cheap attractions that are just as amazing. Potential saving $100.

Drink outdoors with friends
Toronto is super green and the best way to experience the city is to buy a couple of beers from a supermarket and enjoy them somewhere green. A beer costs around $6 in a bar. Potential savings on drinks $50 assuming you have three beers a day - hey you're on vacation!

The secret to saving HUGE amounts of money when travelling to Toronto is...

Your mindset. Money is an emotional topic, if you associate words like cheapskate, Miser (and its £9.50 to go into Charles Dickens London house, oh the Irony) with being thrifty when travelling you are likely to say 'F-it' and spend your money needlessly because you associate pain with saving money. You pay now for an immediate reward. Our brains are prehistoric; they focus on surviving day to day. Travel companies and hotels know this and put trillions into making you believe you will be happier when you spend on their products or services. Our poor brains are up against outdated programming and an onslaught of advertisements bombarding us with the message: spending money on travel equals PLEASURE. To correct this carefully lodged propaganda in your frontal cortex you need to imagine your future self.

Saving money does not make you a cheapskate. It makes you smart. How do people get rich? They invest their money. They don't go out and earn it; they let their money earn more money. So every time you want to spend money, imagine this: while you travel your money is working for you, not you for money. While you sleep the money you've invested is going up and up. That's a pleasure a pricey entrance fee can't give you. Thinking about putting your money to work for you tricks your brain into believing you are not withholding pleasure from yourself, you are saving your money to invest so you can go to even more amazing places. You are thus turning thrifty travel into a pleasure fueled sport.

When you've got money invested - If you want to splash your cash on a first-class airplane seat - you can. I can't tell you how to invest your money, only that you should. Saving $20 on taxi's doesn't seem like much but over time you could be saving upwards of $15,000 a year, which is a deposit for a house which you can rent on Airbnb to finance more travel. Your brain making money looks like your brain on cocaine, so tell yourself saving money is making money.

Scientists have proved that imagining your future self is the easiest way to associate pleasure with saving money. You can download FaceApp — which will give you a picture of what you will look like older and greyer, or you can take a deep breath just before spending money and ask yourself if you will regret the purchase later.

The easiest ways to waste money travelling are:

Getting a taxi. The solution to this is to always download the google map before you go. Many taxi drivers will drive you around for 15 minutes when the place you were trying to get to is a 5-minute walk… remember while not getting an overpriced taxi to tell yourself, 'I am saving money to free myself for more travel.'

Spending money on overpriced food when hungry. The solution: carry snacks. A banana and an apple will cost you, in most places less than a dollar.

Spending on entrance fees to top-rated attractions. If you really want to do it, spend the money happily. If you're conflicted sleep on it. I don't regret spending $200 on a skydive over the Great Barrier Reef, I do regret going to the top of the shard in London for $60. Only you can know but make sure it's your decision and not the marketing directors at said top-rated attraction.

Telling yourself 'you only have the chance to see/eat/experience it now'. While this might be true, make sure YOU WANT to spend the money. Money spent is money you can't invest, and often you can have the same experience for much less.

You can experience luxurious travel on a small budget which will trick your brain into thinking you're already a high-roller, which will mean you'll be more likely to start acting like one and invest your money. Stay in five-star hotels for $5 by booking on the day of your stay on booking.com to enjoy last minute deals. You can go to fancy restaurants using daily deal sites. Ask your airline about last minute upgrades to first-class or business. I paid $100 extra on a $179 ticket to Cuba from Germany to be bumped to Business Class. When you ask you will be surprised what you can get both at hotels and airlines.

Travel, as the saying goes is the only thing you spend money on that makes you richer. In practice, you can easily waste money, making it difficult to enjoy that metaphysical wealth. The biggest money saving secret is to turn bargain hunting into a pleasurable activity, not an annoyance. Budgeting consciously can be fun, don't feel disappointed because you don't spend the $60 to go into an attraction, feel good because soon that $60 will soon be earning money for you. Meaning, you'll have the time and money to enjoy more metaphysical wealth, while your bank balance increases.

So there it is, you can save a small fortune by being strategic with your trip planning. We've arranged everything in the guide to offer the best bang for your buck. Which means we took the view that if it's not a good investment for your money, we wouldn't include it. Why would a guide called 'Super Cheap' include lots of overpriced attractions? That said if you think we've missed something or have unanswered questions ping me an email philgtang@gmail.com I'm on central Europe time and usually reply within 8 hours of getting your mail.

Don't put your dreams off!

Time is a currency you never get back and travel is its greatest return on investment. Plus now you know you can visit Toronto for a fraction of the price most would have you believe. Go and have a fantastic time!

Toronto Streetcar Map

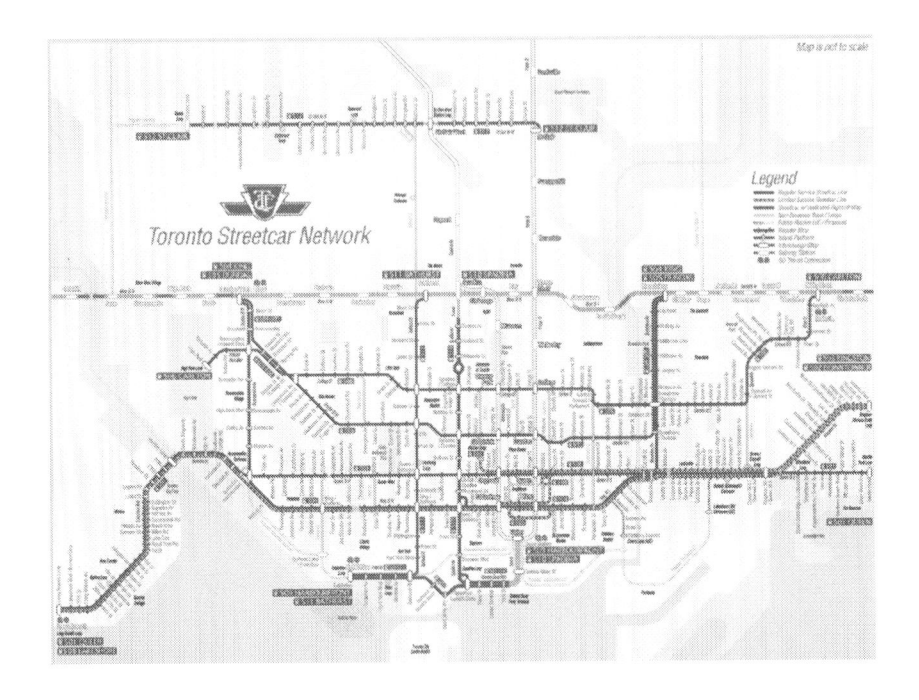

Thank you for reading

Dear Lovely Reader,

If you have found this book useful, please consider writing a short review on Amazon.

One person from every 1000 readers leaves a review on Amazon. It would mean more than you could ever know if you were one of our 1 in 1000 people to take the time to write a short review.

We are a group of four friends who all met travelling 15 years ago. We believe that great experiences don't need to blow your budget, just your mind.

Thank you so much for reading again and for spending your time and investing your trips future in Super Cheap Insider Guides.

Phil

P.S If you need any more super cheap tips we'd love to hear from you e-mail me at philgtang@gmail.com, we have a lot of contacts in every region, so if there's a specific bargain you're hunting we can help you find it :-)

GET 300 TRAVEL GUIDES FULL OF SUPER CHEAP TIPS EXCLUSIVELY AMAZON

UNCOVERED A SUPER CHEAP TIP DURING YOUR TRAVELS? GET PAID FOR IT.
EMAIL PHILGTANG@GMAIL.COM

WE PAY FOR TIPS

CHOOSE FROM PRO RATA ROYALTIES OR A $50 AMAZON VOUCHER

Bonus Budget Travel Hacks

I've included these bonus travel hacks to help you plan and enjoy the trip cheaply, joyfully and smoothly.

How NOT to be ripped off

The thrill of spontaneity is incredible, but if you do a little planning ahead, you will not only save yourself from several mental troubles, but also a lot of money. I am the laziest of planners when it comes to travelling, but I make sure I begin a trip well.

1. **Never ever agree to pay as much as you want trap. Always decide on a price before.**

Whoever you're dealing with is trained to tell you, they are uninterested in money! This is a trap. If you let people do this they will ask for MUCH MORE money at the end, and because you have used there service, you will feel obliged to pay. This is a con-man's trick and nothing more.

2. **Choose to stay in a hostel, instead of a hotel the first nights to get the lay of the land.**

get a chance to learn so much. I have also observed that the location of hostels is often close to main attractions. Also please do not worry about luxury, you are going to spend most of your time outside anyway.

3. **Pack light**

You can move faster and easier. If you take heavy luggage so you will end up taking cabs which are comparatively very costly.

4. **If a local approaches you, they are normally trying to scam you, this is ALWAYS true in tourist destinations.**

5. **Don't book for more than two days and note down the address on your phone**

Unless the place you're doing is going to be busy. e.g Alaska in summer.

6. Withdraw cash from ATM's when you need it, don't carry it with you.

5. NEVER use the airport taxi service. Plan to use public transport before you reach the airport

6. Don't buy a sim card from the airport, but from the local supermarkets it will be 50% less.

7. Eat at local restaurants serving regional food
Food defines culture. Exploring all delights available to the palate.

How to overcome travel related struggles

Anxiety when flying

It has been over 40 years since a plane has been brought down because of turbulence. 40 years! Planes are built to withstand lighting strikes, extreme storms and ultimately can adjust course to get out of their way. Landing and take over are when the most accidents happen, but you have statistically three times the chance of winning a huge jackpot lottery, then you do of crashing then.

If you feel afraid on the flight focus on your breathing saying the word 'smooth' over and over until the flight is smooth. Always check the airline safety record airlinerating.com I was surprised to learn Ryanair and Easyjet as much less safe than Wizz Air according to those ratings. If there is extreme turbulence, I feel much better knowing I'm in a 7 star safety plane.

Wanting to sleep instead of seeing new places

This is a common problem. Just relax, there's little point doing fun things when you feel tired. Plan and fact in jetlag.

Going over budget

Come back from a trip to a monster credit card bill? You're not alone. These are the costs that can crept up. Don't let them.

- To and from the airport. Solution: leave adequate time and take the cheapest method - book before.
- Baggage. Solution: take hand luggage and post things you might need to yourself.
- Eating out. Solution: go to cheap eats places and suggest those to friends.
- Parking. Solution: use apps to find free parking
- Tipping. Solution Leave a modest tip and tell the server you will write them a nice review.
- Souvenirs. Solution: fridge magnets only.
- Giving to the poor. (This one still gets me, but if you're giving away $10 a day - it adds up) Solution: volunteer your time at a local soup kitchens.

Price v Comfort

I love traveling, I don't love struggling. I like decent accommodation, being able to eat properly and see places and enjoy. I am never in the mood for low cost airlines or crappy transfers so here's what I do to save money.

- Avoid organised tours unless you are going to a place where safety is a real issue. They are expensive and constrain your wanderlust to typical things. Note, I only recommend them in Algeria, Iran and Papua New Guinea - where language and gender views pose serious problems all cured by a reputable tour organiser.
- Eat what the locals do.
- Cook in your airbnb/ hostel where restaurants are expensive.
- Shop at local markets.
- Never take the first price.

- Spend time choosing your flight, and check the operator on arilineratings.com
- Mix up hostels and Airbnbs. Hostels for meeting people, Airbnb for relaxing and feeling 'at home'.

Not knowing where toilets are

Use Toilet Finder - https://play.google.com/store/apps/details?id=com.bto.toiletand_hl=en

Your airbnb is awful

Airbnb customer service is notoriously bad. Help yourself out. Never book somewhere without at least 5 reviews. Try to sort things out with the host, but if you can't take photos of everything e.g bed, bathroom, mess, doors, contact them within 24 hours and tell them you had to leave and pay for new accommodation. And ask politely for a full refund.

The airline loses your bag

Take a photo of your checked luggage before you check it.
Go to the Luggage desk before leaving the airport and report the bag missing.
Most airlines will give you an overnight bag, ask where your staying and return the bag to you within three days. Its extremely rare for them to completely lose it these days, but if that happens you should submit an insurance claim.

Your travel companion lets you down.

Whether it's a breakup or a friend cancelling, it sucks and can ramp up costs. In these cases, I normally go to a well-reviewed hostel and find someone I want to travel with - if I need someone to cover the extra costs.

Culture shock

I had one of the strongest culture shocks while spending 6 months in Japan. It was overwhelming how much I actually had to prepare when I went outside of the door (googling words and sentences what to use, where to go, which station and train line to use, what is this food called in Japanese and how does its look etc.). I was so tired constantly but in the end I just let go and went with my extremely bad Japanese. I was trying to ask for soup one day and asked for help with my piles… the people were laughing so hard one actually choked.

If you feel culture shocked its because your brain is referencing your surroundings to what you know. My tip is to just let go and learn some of the local language. You won't like everywhere you go - but you can at least relax everywhere you go.

You're tired

I feel like I just want to go go go go go and See everything and don't let myself just take some time to rest without feeling guilty or conflicted but its important to rest when travelling. I like to create a mini entertainment zone, and occasionally binge watch something or watch documentaries about where I currently am on YouTube.

Car rental

I always use carrentals.com and book with a credit card. Most credit cards will give you free insurance for the car, so you don't need to pay the extra.

You're sick

First off ALWAYS, purchase travel insurance. Including emergency transport up to $500k even to back home, which is usually less than $10 additional. I use https://www.comparethemarket.com/travel-insurance/

If I am sick I normally check into a hotel with room service and ride it out.

Make a Medication Travel Kit

Take medications with you, it is always more expensive to buy there unless you are lucky.

- Antidiarrheal medication (for example, bismuth subsalicylate, loperamide)
- Antihistamine.
- Anti-motion sickness medication.
- Medicine for pain or fever (such as acetaminophen, aspirin, or ibuprofen)
- Mild laxative.
- Cough suppressant/expectorant.
- Throat Lozenges

Save yourself from most travel related hassle

- Do not screw around with immigration and customs staff. You will lose.

- Book the most direct flight you can find, nonstop if possible. Keep weather in mind with connecting flights and watch out for connections in cities with multiple airports through different airports (airlines sometimes connect this way… watch it in places like London and New York)

- Carry a US$ 100 bill for emergency cash. I have entered a country and all ATM and credit card systems were down. US$ can be exchanged nearly anywhere in the world.

- Pack light. Pack light. Pack light. Pack light.

- On long connections, many airport lounges are pay lounges and can be very comfortable and cheaper than a transit hotel.

- Check, and recheck, required visas and such BEFORE the day of your trip. Some countries, for instance, require a ticket out of the country in order to enter. Others, like the US and Australia, require electronic authorization in advance.

- McDonalds and Starbucks offer free wifi in most of the world.

- Security is asinine and inconsistent around the world. Keep this in mind when connecting flights. Always leave at least 2 hours for international connections or international to domestic.

- Expats are rarely the best source for local information. Lots of barstool pontificates in the world.

- Wiki travel is perfect to use for a lay of the land

- Expensive luggage rarely lasts longer than cheap luggage, in my experience. Fancy leather bags are usually toast with air travel.

- Buy travel insurance. A comprehensive annual policy is best and not that expensive.

- Learning to say please and thank you in the local language is not that hard and opens doors. As does a smile and a handshake.

Where and How to Make Friends

Become popular at the airport

Want to become popular at the airport? Pack a power bar with multiple outlets and just see how many friends you make. It's amazing how many people forget their chargers, or who packed them in the luggage that they checked in!

Stay in Hostels

I note there's a line about backpacking, young, confident, hostel demographic that seems to have a whole unspoken backstory going on.

First of all, Hostels don't have to be shared dorms, and they cater to a much wider demographic than is assumed in the OP's comments. In my experience hostels were a way better environment for meeting people than hotels, and more importantly they tended to open up excursion opportunities that further opened up that opportunity. Hotel guests tend to be more cocooned, either couples or families, or if solo, more often than not business travellers, who are rarely interested in chit-chat.

Or take up a hobby

However, if hostels are a definite no-no; find an interest. Take up a hobby where you will meet people. I've dived for years and the nature of diving is you're always paired up with a dive buddy, and I met a lot of interesting people that way. Find something like that the gets people together. However, all of this is about creating the opportunity, you still have to take it, and if you're not the most outgoing person, pack the power supply.

GENERAL HACKS

From saving space in your suitcase to scoring cheap flights, there are a wealth of travel hacks that can help you use to have a stress-free and happy travels without breaking the bank.

Planning and booking stages of travel are equally instrumental in how successful your trip will be, which can be a lot of pressure.

Before You Go

Money

- Get cash from ATMs for best rates.
- Never change at airport exchange desks unless you absolutely have to, then just change enough to get to an ATM.
- Charles Schwab High Yield Checking accounts refund every single ATM fee worldwide, require no minimum balance and have no monthly fee.
- Bring a spare credit card for real emergencies.
- Split cash in various places on your person (pockets, shoes) and in your luggage.
- Use a money belt under your clothes or put $50 in your shoe/ bra incase.

Food

-
- When it comes to food, eat in local restaurants, not tourist-geared joints or choose a hostel.
- with facilities and cook for yourself. The same goes for drinking and going out.

- Bring boiled eggs, canned tuna and nuts with you to avoid being caught out by extreme hunger and having to buy expensive/ unhealthy foods full of sugar.
- Take a spork - a knife, spoon and fork all in one.

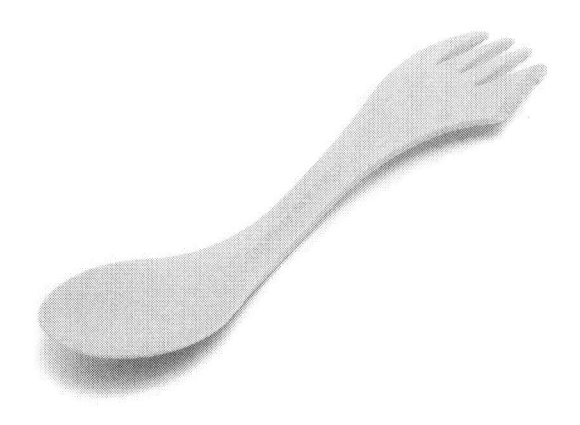

Water Bottle

Take a water bottle with a filter. We love these ones from Water to Go.
Empty it before airport security and seperate the two pieces.

Bug Sprays

Always buy on Amazon. If you have an urgent need while travelling you will pay over the odds. If you are especially tasty to mosquitoes spray your clothes with Permethrin before you travel. A 'Bite Away' zapper can be used after the bite to totally erase it. It cuts down on the itching and need for anti-hestimaines

Order free mini's

Don't buy those expensive travel sized toiletries, order travel sized freebies online. This gives you the opportunity to try brands you've never used before, and who knows, you might even find your new favourite soap.

CHEAP FLIGHT HACKS

Use skyscanner.net - they include the low-cost airlines that others like Kayak leave out.

Use open parameters, e.g if you want to fly from Chicago to Paris, put in USA to France, you may find flights from NYC to Paris for $70 and can take a cheap flight to NYC. Calculate full costs, including accommodation and getting to and from airports before bookting.

ALWAYS USE A PRIVATE BROWSER TO BOOK FLIGHTS

Skyscanner and other sites track your IP address and put prices up and down based on what they determine your desire to buy. e.g if you've booked one-way and are looking for the return these sites will jack the prices up by in most cases 50%. Incognito browsing pays.

Use a VPN such as Hola to book your flight from your destination

Install Hola, change your destination, the location from which a ticket is booked can affect the price. Try using a different address when booking to take advantage of this.

Choose the right time to buy your ticket.

Choose the right time to buy your ticket, as purchasing tickets on a Sunday has been proven to be cheaper. If you can only book during the week, try to do it on a Tuesday.

Fly late for cheaper prices.

Fly late for cheaper prices. Red-eye flights, the ones that leave last in the day, are typically cheaper and less crowded, so aim to book that flight if possible. You will also get through the airport much quicker at the end of the day.

PRO TIP: Get an empty water bottle with you. Once you pass the security check, fill it with water. It will save you $5

Use this APP for same day flights

The Get the Flight Out app (iOS only) from fare tracker Hopper is a go-to choice for travelers looking for same-day flights. The inventory is from major airlines as well as low-cost carriers, and the prices are always favorable. A recent search found a British Airways round-trip from JFK Airport to London's Heathrow for $300.

Take a waterproof bag

If you're travelling alone you can swim without worrying about your phone, wallet and passport laying on the beach.

You can also use it as a source of entertainment on those ultra budget flights

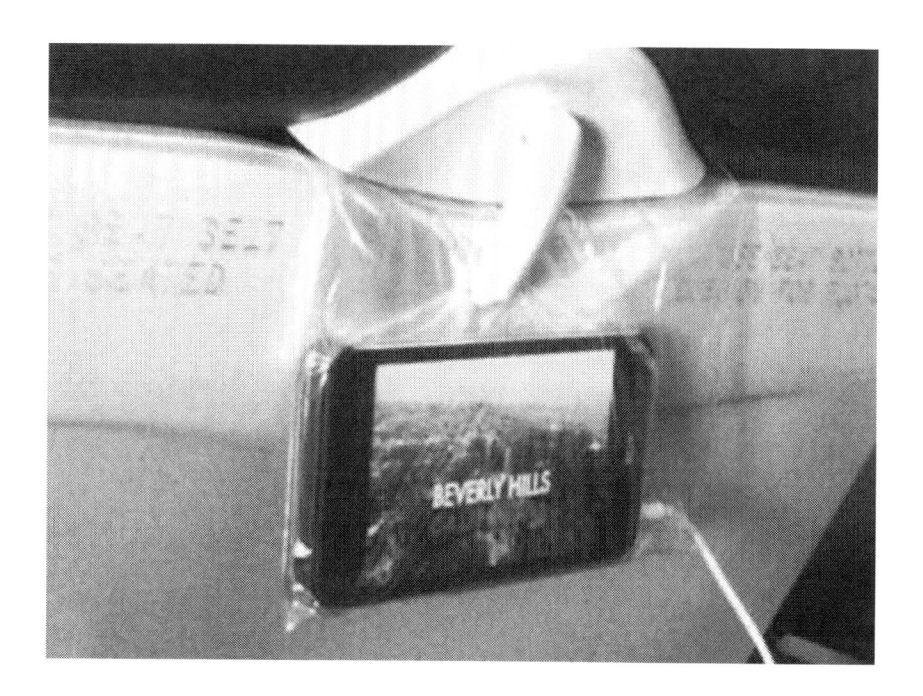

Make a private entertainment centre anywhere

Always take an eye-mask, earplugs, a scarf and a kindle reader - so you can sleep and entertain yourself anywhere!

Take a sponge with you – freeze sponges to keep your food treats fresh.

As long as they are completely frozen, you won't have any problems getting them through airport security.

Travel Gadgets

The door alarm

If you're nervous and staying in private rooms or airbnbs take a door alarm. For those times when you just don't feel safe. 'When you're in a new place, an added measure of protection can give you peace of mind to sleep.

Smart Blanket

I used it when flying to Zurich. The plane was freezing, and there were no blankets to be had. I was the only one that was warm and cozy for the whole 8 hours. Amazon http://amzn.to/2hTYlOP I paid $49.00

The coat that becomes a tent

https://www.adiff.com/products/tent-jacket

Clever Tank Top with Secret Pockets

Keep your valuables safe in this top. Perfect for all climates. https://www.amazon.com/Clever-Travel-Companion-Unisex-secret/dp/B00O94PXLE

Buy on Amazon for $39.90

Convenient Water Bottle with Built-in Pill Organizer

Great way to take your medication while on the go. The medication holder can also be detached. Holding 23 oz. or 600ml, the bottle cap also doubles as a cup. Ingenious!

Optical Camera Lens for Smartphones and Tablets

Leave your bulky camera at home. Turn your device into a high-performance camera. Buy on Amazon for $9.95

Travel-sized Wireless Router with USB Media Storage

Convert any wired network to a wireless network. Buy on Amazon for $17.99

Buy a Scrubba Bag to wash your clothes on the go

Or a cheaper imitable. You can wash your clothes on the go.

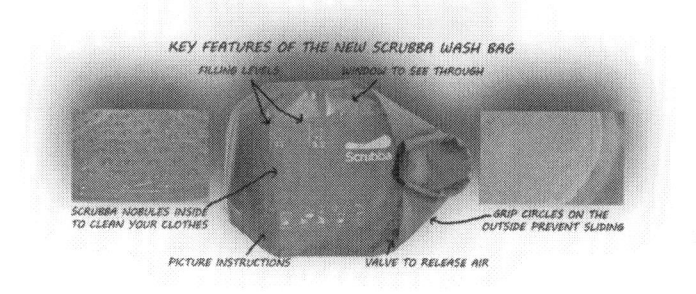

On The Road

Follow locals

Follow the locals. If there are locals around you, you're doing it right. If there are only tourists, you're probably being ripped off.

Set-up a New Uber/ other car hailing app account for discounts

Google offers $50 free for new users in most cities when you have a new gmail.com email account.

Couchsurfing

Totally safe when the person has reviews, but competitive. Book early and confirm before you go. Take a tent, you'll have somewhere to stay if the host cancels last minute.

Hitch-hiking

A good option to save money on transport which will take up a much larger chunk of your budget but only do in groups and let someone know when you are at all times. Family locator app is a good way to do this automatically.

Internet

Check Foursquare for free Wi-Fi hotspots
Get a local cheap sim for data on the go.
Rewards lounges usually have unprotected Wi-Fi networks. Buying Internet access from your mobile device rather than your laptop can get you a better rate. Alternatively, you can spoof your browser's User Agent.

Include external portable power battery for phone charging

Look for people already eating and drinking

Check the Spotted by Locals apps or blogs (Europe and North America)
Get the local experiences: Trip: The Happiest Way to Enjoy Truly Local Experiences (Trip is now available in 86 countries)

Checking Bags

Everyone says this, but it's always worth saying again: Never, ever check a bag if you possibly can avoid it. You're better off doing laundry a couple times in a hostel bathroom. You might also meet interesting people at a coin-op laundry.

Make sure to take a photo of your bag before you check it. This will speed up the paperwork if it is damaged or lost.

Take advantage of other hotel's amenities

Take advantage of other hotel's amenities, for example, if you fancy a swim but you're nowhere near the ocean, try the nearest hotel with a pool. As long as you buy a drink, the hotel staff will likely grant you access.

Fill up your mini bar for free.

Fill up your mini bar for free by storing things from the breakfast bar in your mini bar to give you a greater selection of drinks and food.

Save yourself some ironing

Save yourself some ironing by using the steam from the shower to get rid of wrinkles in clothing. If something is creased, leave it trapped with the steam in the bathroom overnight for even better results.

Recover from a big night out.

Recover from a big night out by using a pants hanger to secure the curtains, keeping your room nice and dark.

See somewhere else for free!

See somewhere else for free! Check to see if your flight offers free stopovers, allowing you to experience another city without spending any extra money.

Wear your heaviest clothes

on the plane to save weight in your suitcase, allowing you to bring more with you. Big coats can then be used as pillows to make your flight more comfortable.

Rebook for a cheaper change of flight.

Some airlines charge high changing fees, whereas last minute flights can be extremely cheap.

Google Your Flight Number before you leave for the airport

Easily find out where your plane is from anywhere. Confirm the status of your flight before you leave.

Protect your belongings during the flight.

Put a 'Fragile' on anything you check to ensure that it's handled better as it goes through security. It'll also be one of the first bags released after the flight, getting you out of the airport quicker.

Don't get lost while you're away.

Find where you want to go using Google Maps, then type 'OK Maps' into the search bar to store this information for offline viewing.

Dine Early

Walk-ins are often accommodated late in the afternoon, and reservations at buzzy restaurants are more plentiful then, too and lunch deals can be half the price of dinner.

Use car renting services

Drive Now or Car2Go.

Share Rides

Use sites like blablacar.com to find others who are driving in your direction. It can be 80% cheaper than normal transport. Just check the drivers reviews.

Use free gym passes

Get a free gym day pass by googling the name of a local gym and free day pass.

When asked by people providing you a service where you are from

If there's no price list for the service you are asking for, when asked where you are from, Say you are from a well-known poorer country. I normally say Macedonia, and if they don't know where it is, add it's a poor country. If you say UK, USA, the majority of Europe bar the well-known poorer countries taxi drivers, tour operators etc will match the price to what they think you pay at home

Hacks for Families

Rent an Airbnb apartment so you can cook

Apartments are much better for families, as you have all the amenities you'd have at home. They are normally cheaper per person too.

Shop at local markets

Eat seasonal products and local products. Get closer to the local market and observe the prices and the offer. What you can find more easily, will be the cheapest

Take Free Tours

Download free podcast tours of the destination you are visiting. The podcast will tell you where to start, where to go, and what to look for. Often you can find multiple podcast tours of the same place. Listen to all of them if you like, each one will tell you a little something new.

Pack Extra Ear Phones

If you go on a museum tour, they often have audio guides. Instead of having to rent one for each person, take some extra earphones. Most audio tour devices have a place to plug in a second set.

Free Hotel Breakfast

Only stay at hotels that include a free breakfast with their standard rate. If you are on a week-long family trip, this could save you a ton of money.

Buy Souvenirs Ahead of Time

If you are buying souvenirs someone touristy, you are paying a premium price. By ordering the same exact products online, you can save a lot of money.

Use Cheap Transportation

Do as the locals do, including weekly passes.

Carry a Reusable Water Bottle

Spending money on water and other beverages can quickly add up. Instead of paying for drinks, take some refillable water bottles.

Combine Attractions

Many major cities offer ticket bundles where one price gets you into 5 or 6 popular attractions. You will need to plan ahead of time to decide what things you plan to do on vacation and see if they are selling these activities together.

Pack Snacks

Granola bars, apples, baby carrots, bananas, cheese crackers, juice boxes, pretzels, fruit snacks, apple sauce, grapes, and veggie chips.

Stick to Carry-On Bags

Do not pay to check a large bag. Even a small child can pull a carry-on.

Visit free art galleries and museums

Just google the name + free days.

Eat Street Food

There's a lot of unnecessary fear around this. You can watch the food prepared. Go for the stands that have a steady queue.

Travel Gadgets for Families

Dropcam

Are what-if scenarios playing out in your head? Then you need Dropcam.

'Dropcam HD Internet Wi-Fi Video Monitoring Cameras help you watch what you love from anywhere. In less than a minute, you'll have it setup and securely streaming video to you over your home Wi-Fi. Watch what you love while away with Dropcam HD.'

Approximate Price: $139

Kelty-Child-Carrier

Voted as one of the best hiking essentials if you're traveling with kids and can carry a child up to 18kg.

Jetkids Bedbox

No more giving up your own personal space on the plane.

How to earn money WHILE travelling

1. Online english teaching job $20 - you will need a private room for this. - https://t.vipkid.com.cn/?refereeId=3262664
2. Work in a hostel. Normally you'll get some cash and free accommodation.
3. Fruit picking. I picked Bananas in Tully Australia for $20 an hour. The jobs are menial but can be quite meditative.
4. You could work on luxury yachts in the med. Its hard work, but you can save money - DesperateSailors.com
5. fiverr.com - offer a small service, like making a video template and changing the content for each buyer.
6. upwork.com - you need to put in a lot of work to make this successful, but if you have a unique skill like coding, or marketing it can be lucrative.
7. Make a udemy.com course
8. Use skype to deliver all manner of services, language lessons, therapy etc. Google for what you could offer. Most speclaisoms have a platform you can use to find clients and they will take a cut of your earnings/ require a fee.
9. Become an Airbnb experience host - but this requires you to know one place and stay there for a time. And you will need a work visa for that country.
10. WWOOF.org which focuses on organic farm work.
11. Rent your place out on airbnb while you travel and get a cleaner to manage it.

Safety

I always check fco.co.uk before travelling. NEVER RELY on websites or books. Things are changing constantly and the FCO's advice is always UP TO DATE and extremely conservative.

I've travelled alone to over 150 countries and the main thing I learnt is if you walk around scared, or anticipating you're going to be pickpocketed, your constant fear will attract bad energy. Murders or attacks on travellers are the mainstay of media, not reality, especially in countries familiar with travellers. The only place I had cause to genuinely fear for my life was Papa New Guinea - where nothing actually happened to me only my own panic over culture shock.

There are many things you can do to stop yourself being victim to the two main problems when travelling: theft or being scammed.

I will address theft first. Here are my top tips. Take these with a pinch of salt, I've written them whilst in India, which can be sketchy if you're travelling alone.

- Stay alert while you're out and always have an exit strategy (no alleyways when alone).
- Keep your money in a few different places on your person and your passport somewhere it can't be grabbed.
- Take a photo of your passport on your phone incase (I never lost of had mine stolen in 15 years of constant travel). If you do lose it, google for your embassy, you can usually get a temporary pretty fast.
- Google safety tips for traveling in your country to help yourself out and memorise the emergency number.
- At hostels keep your large bag in the room far under the bed/ out of the way with a lock on the zipper.

- I keep all money, valuables, passport, etc on me in my day bag. And at night I keep larger bag locked and my day bag in bed next to me/under my pillow depending on how secure the rest of the facilities are. I will alter any of the above based on circumstance or comfortability, for example, the presence of lockers or how many people in the room.
- On buses/trains I would definitely have a lock on the zippers of all bags and I would even lock it to the luggage rack if you want to sleep/if this is a notoriously sketchy route. Bag theft on Indian trains for example is very common.
- I hate constantly checking my bags and having anxiety over it. I bring a small lock for all zippers (with important things not in easily accessible pockets.
- Get a personal keychain alarm. The sound will scare anyone away.
- Don't wear any jewellery. A man attempted to rob a friend of her engagement ring in Bogota, Colombia, and in hindsight I wished I'd told her to leave it at home/wear it on a hidden necklace, as the chaos it created was avoidable.
- Don't hold your phone out while in the street.
- Don't turn your back to traffic while you use your phone.
- When traveling in the tuktuk sit in the middle and keep your bag secure. Wear sunglasses as dust can easily get in your eyes.
- Watch your bag - make sure your zippers are closed and you're aware of your things.
- Don't let anyone give you flowers, bracelets, or any type of trinket, even if they insist it's for free and compliment you like crazy.
- Be careful at night and while drinking.
- Don't go solo on excursions that take you away from crowds.
- Let someone know where you are if you are fearful. Use the family app.
- Don't let strangers know that you are alone - unless they are travel friends ;-) in fact, this is more for avoiding scams or men if you are a women travelling alone.
- Lastly, and most importantly -Trust your gut! If it doesn't feel right, it isn't.

Our Writers

Phil Tang has traveled a number of places using Lonely Planet guides and finds them to be incredibly useful; however, their recommendations for restaurants and accommodation are WAY OUT of my budget. Plus any estimation of cost was always widely inaccurate. So over the past 14 years I started compiling the Super Cheap Insider Guides for people like me, who want a guide within a set budget, but one that doesn't compromise on fun.

Ali Blythe has been writing about amazing places for 17 years. He loves travel and especially tiny budgets equalling big adventures nearly as much as his family. He recently trekked the Satopanth Glacier trekking through those ways from where no one else would trek. A adventure by nature and bargainist by religion, his written over 200 guides for people travelling on a budget.

Michele Whitter writes about languages and travel. What separates her from other travel writers is her will to explain complex topics in a no-nonsense, straightforward manner. She doesn't promise the world. But always delivers step-by-step strategies you can immediately implement to travel on a small Budget.

Kim Mortmier whether it's a two-week, two-month, or two-year trip, Kim's input on Super Cheap Insider Guides Travel Guides show you how to stretch your money further so you can travel cheaper, smarter, and with more wanderlust. She loves going over land on horses.

Copyright

Published in Great Britain in 2019/2020 by Bloom House Press LTD.

Copyright © 2019/2020 Bloom House Press LTD.

The right of Phil G A Tang to be identified as the Author of the Work has been asserted in accordance with the Copyright, Designs and Patents Act 1988.

All rights reserved.

No part of this publication may be reproduced, stored in a retrieval system, or transmitted, in any form or by any means without the prior written permission of the publisher, nor be otherwise circulated in any form of binding or cover other than that in which it is published and without a similar condition being imposed on the subsequent purchaser.

All rights reserved. No part of this publication may be reproduced, distributed, or transmitted in any form or by any means, including photocopying, recording, or other electronic or mechanical methods, without the prior written permission of the publisher, except in the case of brief quotations embodied in critical reviews and certain other non-commercial uses permitted by copyright law.

Our Mission	5
Redefining Super Cheap	11
Discover Toronto	14
Planning your trip	16
Hack your Toronto Accommodation	18
The best price performance location in Toronto	24
Use our FREE	25
accommodation finder service	25
How to be a green tourist in Toronto	27
Saving money on Toronto Food	29
SNAPSHOT: How to Enjoy a $1,000 trip to Toronto for $120	30
Unique bargains I love in Toronto	31
How to use this book	32
OUR super cheap tips	33
Arriving	33
Getting around	34
Start with this free tour	36
See a Blue Jays game on the cheap	38
A cheaper Alternative to the CN Tower	39
Visit these Amazing Free museums	40
Go to the this amazing musical performance for free	42
Take the public ferry	43

Cheap theatre tickets	44
Go to the Beaches	45
Church Hop	46
Go Thrift shopping	47
Explore the BEST markets	49
Pack a picnic	50
Explore Street art	51
Visit this incredible district	52
Watch Free comedy	53
Visit Toronto Eaton Centre	53
Escape the crowds	54
Food and drink tips	55
Not super cheap but worth the fee	57
Is the tap water drinkable?	58
Haggle-o-meter	58
Need to Know	60
Cheapest route to Toronto from America	61
Cheapest route to Toronto from Europe	62
Cheap Eats	63
Avoid these tourist traps or scams	66
Getting Out	67
Personal Cost Breakdown	68
Toronto Streetcar Map	74

Thank you for reading	75
Bonus Budget Travel Hacks	78
How NOT to be ripped off	79
How to overcome travel related struggles	81
Car rental	84
You're sick	85
Where and How to Make Friends	88
GENERAL HACKS	90
CHEAP FLIGHT HACKS	93
Travel Gadgets	96
On The Road	98
Hacks for Families	103
Travel Gadgets for Families	106
How to earn money WHILE travelling	107
Safety	108
Our Writers	110
Copyright	111

HOW DID WE DO?

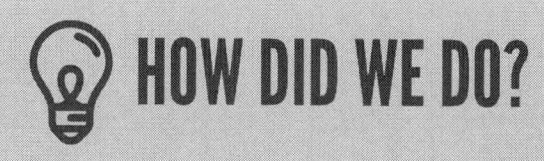

1 DID WE SAVE YOU MONEY?

2 DID YOU LEARN INSIDER INSIGHTS?

3 DID YOU GET A LIST OF THE BEST CHEAP EATS?

4 DID WE HELP YOU PLAN TO SAVE AND ENJOY MORE?

WHAT CAN WE DO BETTER?
EMAIL ME: PHILGTANG@GMAIL.COM

Where NEXT?

ZURICH
VENICE
PRAGUE
MILAN
MARRAKESH
AUSTIN
CAPPADOCIA
EDINBURGH
ANTARCTICA

SUPERCHEAPINSIDERGUIDES.COM

Printed in Great Britain
by Amazon